T0188534

RECYCLE
AND
REMAKE

New things from old trash

The activities in this book are designed to help you make stuff from things that you might otherwise throw out. You will find the list of things you can rescue from the trash at the start of each project in the "from the garbage" section. Collect your materials from what you already have at home and give them a cleaning before you use them. Please don't buy new garbage to make the projects in this book!

Look out for this warning sign. It shows where you will need grown-up help.

DK | Penguin Random House

Editor Hélène Hilton
Project Art Editor Charlotte Bull
Designer Sadie Thomas
Additional Illustration Kitty Glavin
US Editor Mindy Fichter
US Senior Editor Shannon Beatty
Photographer Ruth Jenkinson
Fact Checker Lizzie Davey
Managing Editor Penny Smith
Managing Art Editor Mabel Chan
Producers, Pre-Production Sophie Chatellier, Abigail Maxwell
Producer Amy Knight
Picture Researcher Sakshi Saluja
Jacket Designer Rachael Parfitt Hunt
Jacket Co-ordinator Issy Walsh
Publishing Director Sarah Larter
Creative Director Helen Senior

First American Edition, 2020
Published in the United States by DK Publishing
1450 Broadway, Suite 801, New York, NY 10018

Copyright © 2020 Dorling Kindersley Limited
DK, a Division of Penguin Random House LLC
21 22 23 10 9 8 7 6 5 4 3 2
009–315391–Mar/2020

A catalog record for this book
is available from the Library of Congress.
ISBN 978-1-4654-8984-5

DK books are available at special discounts when purchased in bulk for sales promotions, premiums, fund-raising, or educational use. For details, contact: DK Publishing Special Markets, 1450 Broadway, Suite 801, New York, NY 10018
SpecialSales@dk.com

Printed and bound in China

A WORLD OF IDEAS:
SEE ALL THERE IS TO KNOW

www.dk.com

Contents

Planet health check

The Earth is our home. However, we humans don't always take care of it properly. Understanding what we do wrong can help us fix it.

Wherever humans go, we change the natural environment. We've even left garbage in space! To keep our planet healthy, we need to clean up after ourselves.

Landfills are huge places where garbage is dumped then covered up or buried.

No such thing as "away"

When you throw something out, it doesn't really go away. Most garbage is burned or dumped in a landfill, but some can be recycled. Recycling means making waste into something new!

Plastic pollution

Plastic waste takes thousands of years to break down into tiny pieces. Unwanted plastic can hurt animals that get caught in it or eat it accidentally.

Food waste

Growing food for everyone on Earth takes up a lot of space and energy. On top of this, huge amounts of food are thrown away uneaten.

Global warming

Technology, factories, and vehicles need energy to work. Making this energy releases gases into the air that trap the sun's heat. This means the planet is getting hotter and much harder to live on.

Fading forests

The world's forests are being cut down and burned to make room for cities and farms. Trees clean the gases that add to global warming. Without forests, the planet will get even hotter.

Life on Earth

As humans damage nature, other animals and plants struggle. Many are in danger of dying out altogether, and becoming extinct.

Let's heal the planet

Together, we can save the planet! The activities in this book are a good start. By giving trash a new life, you'll be reducing waste in the world.

The plastic problem

Plastic is very useful! We use it for everything from straws to buildings. The problem is that once it's made, plastic never really goes away.

Oil pump

Where does plastic come from?

Most plastic is made from oil, which takes millions of years to form deep inside the Earth. Oil is drilled out from under the ground or under the sea.

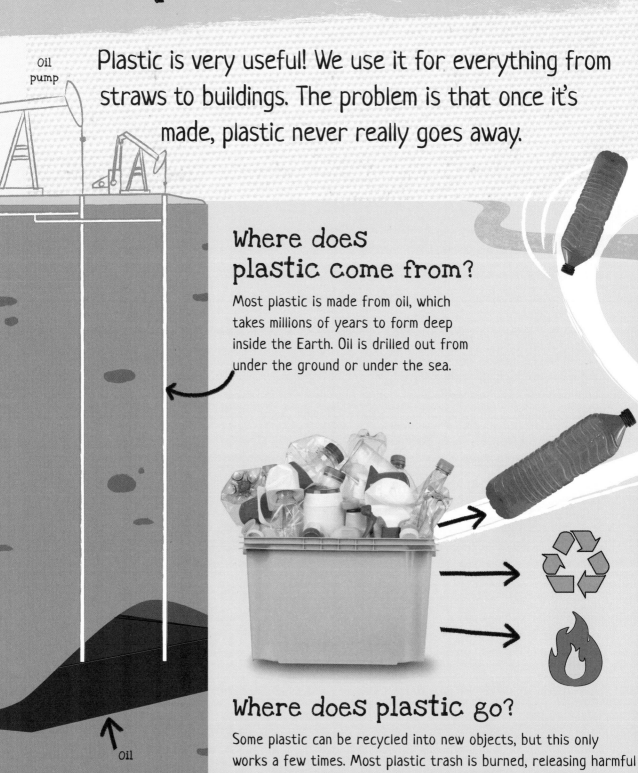

Oil

Where does plastic go?

Some plastic can be recycled into new objects, but this only works a few times. Most plastic trash is burned, releasing harmful gases into the air. Some is dumped in landfills or at sea.

Sea of plastic

A lot of plastic ends up in the seas and oceans, either by accident or because people dump it there. Sea animals such as dolphins, birds, and turtles can get caught in it.

Put garbage in the can to stop it from being blown into rivers and the sea.

Sea birds and other animals have been found with plastic in their stomachs. Swallowing plastic hurts them from the inside. It also doesn't leave room in their stomachs for real food, so they die.

Scientists are inventing alternatives to plastic. For example, they have made water pods from seaweed that could replace plastic bottles.

Plastic planters

Don't throw out all your plastic bottles! Try turning them into new homes for your favorite plants.

What will you put in your planter? See pages 32 and 33 to learn how to make your own compost.

From the garbage
Plastic bottles

Extra supplies
Scissors

Acrylic paint

Paintbrushes

String

1

Save the middle part! You can use it to make a bee hotel on the next page.

⚠️

Cut the top and the bottom off a bottle. Both pieces can be used to make planters.

2

Decorate the planters by painting on a pattern or picture. You might need more than one coat of paint to make the colors pop!

For hanging planters, use scissors to make two or three holes around the rim of the planter. Knot string through each hole, then hang from a hook.

⚠️

9

Welcome to the Bee Hotel!

Make a bee-rilliant hotel to get your garden or local park buzzing with life! Look in your trash to help you decide which of these bee hotels to make.

Hang up your hotel somewhere sheltered from the rain and wind.

From the garbage

Old plant pots

Dry grass

Newspaper or scrap paper

Cardboard

Bamboo canes

Extra supplies

Scissors

String

Vacancies!

Different types of bees need different sized bedrooms.

Collect plant pots that are no longer needed.

Fill a plant pot with bamboo canes left over from crafting.

Roll up pieces of newspaper or scrap paper to make little bee-sized tubes.

Find a quiet spot in a garden or park to leave your bee hotel.

Make sure the paper rolls are packed in tightly so they don't blow away.

How do bees help the planet?

Bees are pollinators—they buzz from flower to flower, spreading pollen. When a flower receives pollen, it can make seeds, which then grow into new plants. Without bees, many plants would disappear.

Roll up cardboard in a swirl. Fill the gaps with dry grass so it doesn't move around.

Rescued pencil cups

Rescue a used plastic cup from the garbage! You can turn it into a colorful pencil holder.

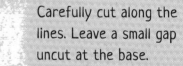

Try weaving strips of plastic bags.

1 Ask a grown-up to help you measure the side of the cup with a ruler and draw lines to divide it into sections.

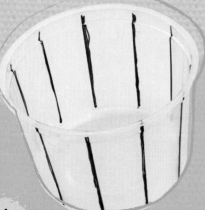

Split the cup into an odd number of sections, such as 7, 9, 11, or 13 sections.

2 Carefully cut along the lines. Leave a small gap uncut at the base.

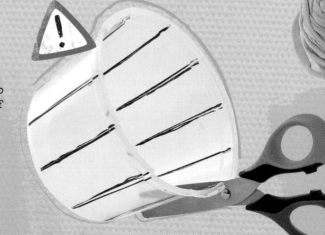

Make a braid

Tie three lengths of fabric into a knot at one end. Move the outer color over the top and between the other two. Take turns moving the left color and the right color into the middle until the braid is long enough, then tie it off.

Keep practicing!

Glue braids to the top and bottom to decorate.

3 Tie a knot in the end of your fabric and push it between two sections. Weave it in and out of the sections around the cup.

4 Keep weaving until you get to the top! To finish, or to change color, tie a little knot in your fabric inside the cup.

Push the fabric down as you go.

Planet of trees

Trees provide homes for animals, clean the air we breathe, and keep our planet healthy. However, forests around the world are disappearing.

Forests are home to plants and animals that can live nowhere else. As the forests are cut down, some plants and animals will disappear forever.

Plants take in carbon dioxide gas from the air and turn it into oxygen. Carbon dioxide traps heat, making our planet hotter. By using it, trees help fight the climate crisis.

Trees soak up water when it rains, and release any they don't need through their leaves as water vapor. This helps keep the air cool.

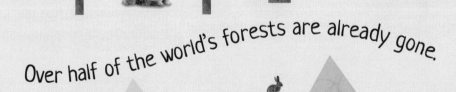

Over half of the world's forests are already gone.

The main reason forests are destroyed is to make space for towns and farms.

Growing on trees

We use things from trees every day. Many of our favorite fruits and most important medicines come from trees. Wood, from a tree's trunks and branches, is a great material to make homes, furniture, paper, and cardboard.

To make paper or cardboard from a tree, wood is chopped up into tiny pieces and mixed with water. This makes pulp, which is then dried into sheets of paper or board.

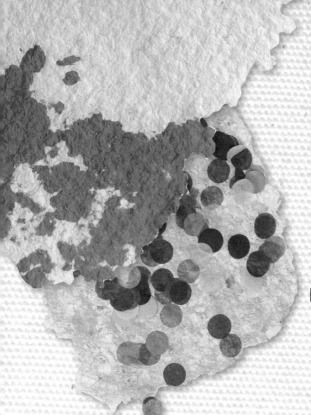

Recycled bookmarks

Save trees by making your very own recycled paper. Once you've mashed the paper up into a pulp, you can dry it into sheets and cut it into bookmarks.

From the garbage

Scrap paper (newspaper, used gift wrap, or junk mail)

Extra supplies

Bowl

Warm water

Tray

Cloth napkin

Decorations (petals, hay, confetti)

Sponge

Scissors

Ribbon

1 Start breaking down your scrap paper by ripping it up into little pieces into a bowl.

2

Pour warm water into the bowl, covering the paper, and let it soak for around half an hour.

Squeeze!

3

It's time to get messy! Squeeze and rip the soaked paper until it feels gooey. Paper mush is called pulp.

Squish!

Mash!

Turn the page to make sheets of paper.

Tip!
For rainbow sheets, make pulp from scrap paper of different colors.

4

Cloth napkin

Pour a thin layer of pulp into a tray over a cloth napkin. Add decoration to the pulp if you like, then fold the cloth over the top. Sponge up the water through the cloth, squishing the pulp as you go.

Paper pulp

Soak up the water.

Squish!

Press!

5

Leave the sheet to dry for a couple of days, then gently lift it out of the tray.

Seeded shapes

If you have leftover pulp, you can make little seeded shapes with it. Place the pulp inside a cookie cutter and push it up to the edges.

Gently lift the cutter away, squish on some seeds, then leave the shapes to dry for a few days.

Plant the seeded shapes in soil and compost, then water. The paper will break down and the seeds will slowly grow.

6 Cut your new sheets into bookmarks. Add a ribbon to make an extra fancy bookmark!

What decorations will you add? You could try flower petals, hay, or confetti.

Two things to make with
a shoe box

A shoe box isn't just great to store shoes in. Here are two fun games you could make.

I want to play!

Bead maze

Turn the **shoe box lid** into a maze! Move the lid from side to side to roll the beads from start to finish.

Start here

Make the maze walls from pieces of scrap cardboard or old straws. Stick them in place with tape or glue.

End here

You could try painting your maze and beads.

Shadow theater

Use the **base of the shoe box** to make a mini shadow puppet theater. What story will you tell?

Make character puppets from black cardboard and sticks to use in your theater.

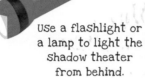

Use a flashlight or a lamp to light the shadow theater from behind.

parchment paper

Carefully cut a rectangle out of the bottom of the box. Stick parchment paper to the inside.

Tip! Decorate your theater with painted cardboard curtains.

Cardboard castle

With a little imagination, you can turn a boring old cardboard box into something completely magical.

1 Draw these shapes on cardboard with a ruler. The bigger you make them, the bigger your castle will be!

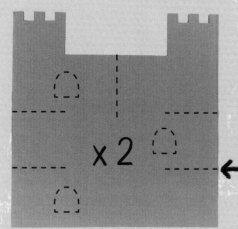

These two pieces will be the front and back walls of your castle.

These slits should be the same thickness as the cardboard.

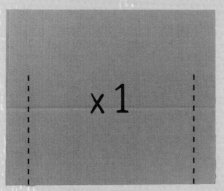

This piece will be the middle wall.

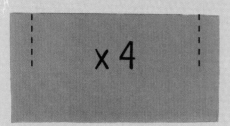

These four pieces will be the castle's floors.

2 ⚠ Cut out the castle shapes, windows, and slits along the dotted lines. Paint on extra decorations if you want.

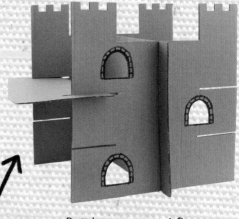

3 Build your castle! Start with the middle and outer walls, then add the floors.

From the garbage

Cardboard boxes

Extra supplies

Ruler

Scissors

Paint and paintbrushes

Get that dragon!

Ahhhh!

Time to play!

23

Party piñata

Make this special party game from a cardboard box. It doesn't need to be very neat, since you'll soon be bashing it open to get to the tasty treasure inside!

From the garbage
Cardboard boxes
Used wrapping paper

Extra supplies
Pen
Scissors
Ruler
Masking tape
Candy (foil or paper-wrapped candies are best)
String

Tip!
Most plastic sticky tape can't be recycled. Use paper masking tape to make your piñata so you can recycle it after your party.

1

Draw the shape of your piñata on the cardboard and carefully cut it out. Draw around the cutout to make a second, identical shape and cut that out, too.

2

Use a ruler to draw long rectangles on another piece of cardboard and cut them out. These will be the sides of the piñata.

3

Stick the strips all the way around to the edges of the shape with tape. Bend the cardboard to fit the shape and trim any pieces that are too long.

4

Fill the piñata with candy! Then stick the lid down with more tape.

5

Cut strips of old wrapping paper. Snip little notches in the paper to make it ruffly.

6

Decorate your piñata by sticking the ruffly paper on in layers using more tape. Keep going until you can't see the cardboard.

7 ⚠ Ask a grown-up to poke a hole in the piñata to hang it up. Use strong string since it's about to get bashed!

Party time!

Take turns with your party guests bashing the piñata with a soft bat! Be careful not to hit your friends.

Add streamers if you have extra wrapping paper.

Once the piñata breaks open, all the candies will tumble out!

Fresh from the farm

There are nearly eight billion people on the planet, and they all need to eat! We need to think carefully about how we can grow enough food without harming the Earth.

Clearing forests

Farming is the main reason forests are being burned and cut down. Humans clear trees to make fields for farm animals to live in and to grow animal feed. Space is also cleared to grow crops, such as palm trees for palm oil.

Palm oil is used in a lot of prepared foods and products, such as bread and toiletries.

Palm oil is called many different names, including vegetable oil, vegetable fat, and glyceryl.

Palm oil farm

Homegrown food

Food grown on the other side of the world is often transported to other countries by plane or boat, which pollutes the air and sea. Check labels to find food that was grown locally, or try to grow your own.

Eat more vegetables!

Farm animals need a lot of space, water, and energy to feed and grow. Humans can help the planet by eating more plants and less meat, so we don't need as many farm animals.

Try some tasty new plant-based recipes!

Cows fart out a gas called methane, which contributes to global warming. Unfortunately, cows fart a lot...and there are more than a billion of them in the world.

More than half of all the mammals in the world are farm animals, such as cows and sheep. Humans make up another third. Less than one in every twenty mammals in the world is a wild animal.

Chemical farming

Farmers often use chemicals, such as fertilizers and pesticides, to help their plants grow. These chemicals can poison plants and animals. They also get into rivers and seas. That's why other farmers choose to use fewer or no chemicals.

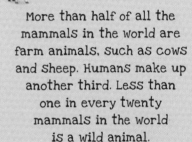

Seven out of every ten birds in the world are farm birds, such as chickens.

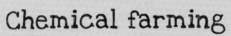

New plants from food scraps

Instead of throwing out your food scraps, give your fruits and vegetables a chance at an exciting new life.

Celery

Celery will grow new crunchy stalks if it gets plenty of water and sunshine.

Garlic

Suspend a garlic clove in water with toothpicks. Within a few days it should sprout a stem and little roots. Plant it in soil and compost to regrow a whole new garlic bulb.

Carrots

Carrot tops won't grow new carrots, but they can grow new leaves. Place them in the sun in a shallow dish of water. Once the leaves start to grow, plant the carrot tops in soil and compost to make a pretty potted plant.

what do plants need to live?

Plants need light and water. They use their leaves to soak up light from the sun. They suck up water from the soil around their roots.

Lettuce

Lettuce will grow new leaves if you leave the stem in a little water in a sunny place.

Spring onions

Save your spring onion roots to regrow them. Set them up in a glass of water, then plant them in soil and compost once the roots have started to grow.

Fruits have seeds, pits, or stones inside them. These are what new plants can grow from. Plant different seeds in soil and compost to see what happens!

Avocados

Avocados have a big, round pit inside of them. Suspend one in water until it grows a root and a leafy stem. Plant it in soil and compost. After a few years you will have an avocado tree.

31

Food for plants

Some food scraps are no good for us to eat, but we can use them in other ways. Break them down into compost. Compost is a superfood for plants!

In your compost

For your compost to break down properly, you'll need the right mix of "brown" and "green" things. Try to use about half-and-half "brown" and "green" waste.

Paper and newspaper

Dry sticks and leaves

These count as "brown" things.

Cardboard

Dry grass

To make your compost, you'll need a compost bin in your backyard or a mini compost bin on your balcony. Pick a sheltered place in the shade.

Little bugs might come and live in your compost. They help to break it down.

Potato peelings

Apple skin

Green leaves and grass

Banana skins

These count as "green" things.

Fruit peelings

Vegetables peelings

Wait a few months for the scraps to break down. The compost should be brown, without any pieces in it. Mix your compost with soil to help new plants grow.

Eggshell seed cups

Empty eggshells work well as tiny, natural plant pots. Use your homemade compost, too, to grow something new.

Extra supplies

Compost and soil

Spoon

Seeds

Water

Plant pot or jar

1 Fill the eggshells with a mix of soil and compost. Pat it down, leaving a little space at the top.

2 Carefully sprinkle the seeds over the soil.

Seeds

Soil

3 Cover the seeds with a little more soil and compost, then gently pat down again.

How do plants help the Earth?

Plants don't breathe like we do, but they do take in an invisible gas called carbon dioxide from the air. Carbon dioxide makes the planet hotter, which is bad for the environment. Growing more plants helps to fight against global warming and the climate crisis!

4 Place your eggs in a sunny place. Water the soil, then wait.

Repot other plants in jars of soil, such as your spring onion scraps from page 31.

5

within a day or two, you should see little green shoots.

When the shoots appear, gently crack the eggshell, then place the whole thing in a bigger pot of soil and compost. The shell will break down and feed your plant, and the roots will grow through the little cracks.

Our clothes

Have you ever thought about where your clothes come from or how they were made? The clothes we buy have a big impact on our planet.

Take a look at the label on your clothing. What material is it made from?

What is fabric?

Fabric is what clothes are made from. It can be made from man-made materials or natural things like plants.

Man-made fabrics, such as polyester, are usually made of plastic. When these fabrics are washed, tiny bits of plastic fall off and are carried away to the ocean.

Natural fabrics, such as cotton, are made from plants, which can need a lot of water to grow.

To get the most out of your clothes, wear them until you grow out of them. You can also use fabric from damaged clothes to make something new.

Too much to wear

Billions of clothes are made every year, but not all are sold and many are thrown away. Some people also throw out their clothes when they get bored of them.

Picked cotton

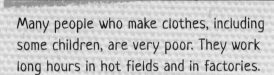

Many people who make clothes, including some children, are very poor. They work long hours in hot fields and in factories.

Cotton

What happens to the clothes?

Clothes that are trashed often end up in the landfill. Instead of throwing away clothes that are too small, give them to other people who will wear them, or to a resale store. That way fewer new clothes will need to be made.

Wax wrap

Cheer up your snack with this colorful beeswax food wrap. Use it instead of plastic wrap to reduce waste. You can reuse it over and over again!

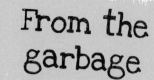

From the garbage
Scrap piece of cotton fabric

Extra supplies
Ironing board
Parchment paper
Beeswax bars
Cheese grater
Iron
Scissors
String (to tie up your wrap)

1

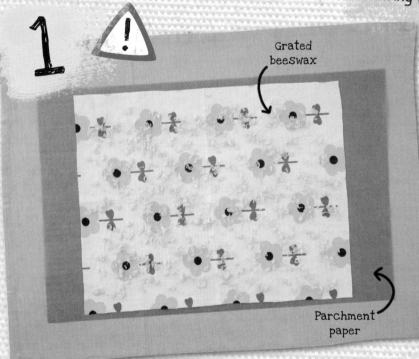

Grated beeswax

Parchment paper

Put the cotton on an ironing board, on top of a sheet of parchment paper. Carefully grate beeswax onto the cotton, leaving space around the edges.

Beeswax bars

2

Place a second sheet of parchment paper on top. Ask a grown-up to help you iron the cotton until you can see the wax melting into it.

!

3

Leave the wrap to cool, then peel it off the parchment paper.

!

Cut off the unwaxed edges of your wrap.

Start wrapping your lunches and snacks! When your wrap gets dirty, wipe it clean with a sponge.

Three things to make with
fabric scraps

Even if you take really good care of your clothes, they will eventually get worn out. You can turn any fabric scrap into something cool.

Denim pencil cup

If your jeans get too short, cut the legs off and turn them into shorts. Then use the legs to make these little cups.

Turn the cut-off leg inside out. Bunch up one end, then tie it off with an elastic band. Turn the leg back right side out, tucking the bunched up end inside.

Roll down the top of the pencil cup to help it stand up.

Friendship bracelet

Cut some skinny strips of fabric to braid into colorful friendship bracelets. Choose your favorite colors, your team colors, or just colors that look nice together.

Look at page 13 to remind yourself how to do a braid, then tie the ends around your wrist with a knot.

Some people say that if you wear a friendship bracelet until it falls off, your wish will come true!

Forever bangle

To make a fancy bracelet, use an old plastic bottle and fabric scraps to make a bangle. This way, you're recycling two things at once!

Cut a ring out of a plastic bottle. Wrap fabric scraps around the ring, tucking the end under as you go. If it doesn't stay, glue the fabric to stop it from unraveling. Keep wrapping until you can't see the plastic anymore.

41

Favorite tote bag

If your favorite T-shirt is wearing out, turn it into a great tote bag! Carry it around in a pocket so you never have to use a plastic carrying bag again.

1 Cut the arms off your T-shirt to make the handles. Cut a semicircle off under the neck.

These will be the bag's handles.

From the garbage
An old T-shirt

Extra supplies
Scissors

2 Turn the T-shirt inside out. Snip slits along the bottom, leaving long thin strips of fabric that you can tie into knots.

3 Work your way along the bottom tying the fabric strips into double knots. This will bring the sides of the T-shirt together.

Zero-waste stores are places where you can buy groceries without any packaging. Shoppers bring their own reusable bags and containers to cut down on waste.

What will you fill

your bag with?

4 Turn the T-shirt the right side out and enjoy your new bag!

It's an emergency!

Global warming is the biggest challenge facing our planet. The Earth is steadily getting hotter, and as humans burn more energy this is happening faster and faster.

We can save the planet!

Burning energy

A lot of the energy we use to make things work comes from burning oil and coal. They are burned to make electricity and used as fuel for cars and planes. This releases gases, such as carbon dioxide, that trap heat close to the planet.

To stop the Earth from getting hotter, we have to cut down on harmful gases. We should also plant a lot more trees to get rid of the extra carbon dioxide already in the air.

Clean energies

The power of sunlight, wind, and moving water can also make electricity. These are clean energies because they don't harm the planet.

Global crisis

Even if the Earth is getting hotter, the weather where you are might not change that much. Global warming affects the world overall, even if you can't see it yourself.

As weather becomes more extreme, there are more droughts and fires, and also more floods.

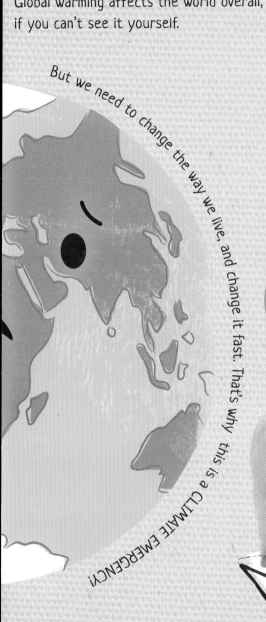

But we need to change the way we live, and change it fast. That's why this is a CLIMATE EMERGENCY!

Ice that hasn't melted for millions of years is melting now. If it continues, sea levels will rise and flooded land will disappear into the sea.

Animals like polar bears that need ice to live on have nowhere to go and can't find food.

The seas are also heating up. Even getting a little bit hotter kills coral reefs, which provide homes for billions of animals.

Throughout the world, many people are working very hard to save the planet. **Turn to the next page to see what you can do!**

Little changes make a big difference

Switch lights off
to save electricity.

Earth is the only planet where humans, animals, and plants can live. Here are some ways you and your family can help take care of it.

walk, bicycle, or take the bus to

Check that the energy you use at home is clean and green.

Eat less meat and dairy to reduce the space and water used for farming.

Plant a tree to fight global warming.

Really think about the things you buy. How and where were they made? Do you really need to buy more?

Work together

There are a lot of things you can do by yourself, but we can do even more together. Make your voice heard by writing to politicians who can make big changes, or join an environmental group with your family.

cut down on car pollution.

Take the train instead of flying to make less carbon dioxide.

Choose natural fabrics and wash your clothes less often to stop tiny pieces of plastic from getting into the ocean.

Buy secondhand to reuse, rather than buying new things.

Wash clothes at a lower temperature to save energy.

Turn things off

instead of leaving them on standby, which saves electricity.

Use reusable containers such as cups, jars, and bags to cut out single-use plastic.

Index

DK would like to thank

Becky Walsh, Brandie Tully-Scott, and Celine Ka Wing Lau for craft and photoshoot assistance, James Mitchem and Seeta Parmar for editorial help.

Acknowledgments

The publisher would like to thank the following for their kind permission to reproduce their photographs:

(Key: a-above; b-below/bottom; c-center; f-far; l-left; r-right; t-top)

2-3 DreamStime.com: Praewpailin PhonSri (Background). **3 Fotolia:** Eric ISSelee (bl). **4 Alamy Stock Photo:** Jupiterimages (cra). **DreamStime.com:** Alfio Scisetti / Scisettialfio (br); Vchalup (cl). **iStockphoto.com:** Robert Pleško (bl). **4-5 DreamStime.com:** Praewpailin PhonSri (Background). **5 Fotolia:** Eric ISSelee (cr). **6-7 DreamStime.com:** Praewpailin PhonSri (Background). **6 DreamStime.com:** Photka (cb); Alfio Scisetti / Scisettialfio (cra, crb). **7 123RF.com:** (clb/Ban Sign); AlekSey Poprugin (bc). **Alamy Stock Photo:** Paulo Oliveira (tr). **Dorling KinderSley:** Natural History MuSeum, London (clb). **DreamStime.com:** Onyxprj (clb/Plastic bottles); Alfio Scisetti / Scisettialfio (cla, cl, c, cb). **10-11 DreamStime.com:** Praewpailin PhonSri (Background). **14 DreamStime.com:** Galyna Andrushko (cla). **Fotolia:** Eric ISSelee (cb). **14-15 DreamStime.com:** Praewpailin PhonSri (Background). **15 123RF.com:** Eric ISSelee / isselee (clb); PicSfive (crb). **DreamStime.com:** Damian Palus (fclb); Yotrak (tr). **16-17 DreamStime.com:** Praewpailin PhonSri (Background). **18-19 DreamStime.com:** Praewpailin PhonSri (Background). **20 DreamStime.com:** OlekSandr Shyripa (cra). **20-21 DreamStime.com:** Praewpailin PhonSri (Background). **21 Fotolia:** Matthew Cole (ca). **22-23 DreamStime.com:** Praewpailin PhonSri (Background).

24-25 DreamStime.com: Praewpailin PhonSri (Background). **26-27 DreamStime.com:** Praewpailin PhonSri (Background). **28-29 DreamStime.com:** Praewpailin PhonSri (Background). **28 DreamStime.com:** Grafner (crb). iStockphoto.com: Yusnizam (cb). **29 123RF.com:** Eric ISSelee / isselee (cl, cra, ca, cb, cr); Sauletas (clb). **DreamStime.com:** Ekaterina Semenova / EkaterinaSemenova (tl). **32-33 DreamStime.com:** Praewpailin PhonSri (Background). **34-35 DreamStime.com:** Praewpailin PhonSri (Background). **36-37 DreamStime.com:** Praewpailin PhonSri (Background). **iStockphoto.com:** Foto-Ianniello (c). **37 DreamStime.com:** Gillespaire (tr). **iStockphoto.com:** Neenawat (cr). **38-39 DreamStime.com:** Praewpailin PhonSri (Background). **40-41 DreamStime.com:** Praewpailin PhonSri (Background). **42-43 DreamStime.com:** Praewpailin PhonSri (Background). **44-45 DreamStime.com:** Praewpailin PhonSri (Background). **44 123RF.com:** AlphaSpirit (br). **iStockphoto.com:** Plherrera (cl). **45 Dorling KinderSley:** Jerry Young (cb). **iStockphoto.com:** Milehightraveler (tr). **46 123RF.com:** Eric ISSelee / isselee (clb, cb). **46-47 DreamStime.com:** Praewpailin PhonSri (Background). **47 123RF.com:** Natthawut Panyosaeng / aopsan (br). **DreamStime.com:** Gv1961 (cra). **48 DreamStime.com:** Praewpailin PhonSri (Background).

Cover images: Front: **123RF.com:** RoyStudio, Roman Samokhin ca; Back: **123RF.com:** RoyStudio

All other images © Dorling KinderSley
For further information See: www.dkimages.com